YOUNG RESEARCHER

THE NORMANS

Hazel Mary Martell

© Heinemann Educational Books Ltd

First published in 1992 by
Heinemann Children's Reference,
a division of Heinemann Educational Books Ltd,
Halley Court, Jordan Hill, Oxford OX2 8EJ.

OXFORD LONDON EDINBURGH
MADRID PARIS ATHENS BOLOGNA
MELBOURNE SYDNEY AUCKLAND SINGAPORE
TOKYO IBADAN NAIROBI GABORONE HARARE
PORTSMOUTH NH (USA)

Designed by Julian Holland Publishing Ltd
Picture Research by Ann-Marie Ehrlich
Colour artwork by Gecko and Martin Smillie
Editorial planning Jackie Gaff

Printed in Hong Kong

British Library Cataloguing in Publication Data

Martell, Hazel Mary
  The Normans. − (Young researcher)
  I. Title II. Series
  942.02

ISBN 0-431-00569-9

Photographic acknowledgements

The authors and publishers wish to acknowledge with thanks, the following photographic sources:
a = above b = below c = centre l = left r = right
Aerofilms 31*l*; Ancient Art and Architecture Collection 33*a*, 35*r*, 36*a*, 42, 51, 58; Bodleian Library 13*l*; 15, 19*l*, 20*l*, 33*c*, 35*l*, 39*b*, 41*b*, 43, 45*a*; Bodleian Library/University College 43*r*; British Library 11*l*, 22, 23*b*, 27*r*, 30, 32*r*, 39, 41*a*, 53*r*; British Museum 13*r*; C.M. Dixon 14, 17*r*, 46, 54; E T Archive 8 9*r*, 10, 44, 59*b*; Sonia Halliday 27*l*; 48*l*; Clive Hicks 19*r*, 25*r*, 28, 31*r*; Michael Holford 5, 9*l*, 23*a*, 36*c*, 40, 50, 55, 56, 57, 59*a*; A. F. Kersting 4, 24, 53*l*; Museum of London 6, 7*r*, 12, 32*l*, 17*l*, 38; Skyscan 7*l*; The Master and Fellows of Trinity College Cambridge 45*b*; Victoria and Albert Museum 25*l*; Visionbank 34.
The publishers have made every effort to trace the copyright holders, but if they have inadvertently overlooked any, they will be pleased to make the necessary arrangement at the first opportunity.

Note to the reader
In this book there are some words in the text which are printed in **bold** type. This shows that the word is listed in the glossary on page 62. The glossary gives a brief explanation of words which may be new to you.

Contents

Who were the Normans?

The Normans were a group of people who lived in north western France more than 1000 years ago. Their ancestors were the Vikings from Norway and Denmark who raided France in the ninth century. The word *Norman* came from *Norseman,* a **medieval** word for a Viking. At first the kings of France gave the Vikings money to go away. In 911, however, King Charles the Simple made a **treaty** with a Viking chief called Hrolf, or Rollo. This allowed Rollo and his followers to settle in the part of France that became known as the **Duchy** of Normandy. In return, they had to defend France against other Viking attacks. Rollo became **Duke** of Normandy. When he died the title passed to his son, William.

The Normans spread out

In the eleventh century, the Normans conquered southern Italy and Sicily. In 1062 William, a great-great-grandson of Rollo, added Maine to his territory in France. Then in 1066 William conquered England. From there the Norman influence spread to Wales, Scotland and Ireland.

△ **A Norman warrior.** This is the tomb of Robert Curthose, the eldest son of William the Conqueror. Like most Normans, he enjoyed fighting. He invaded England in 1101 because he thought he should be king. His youngest brother Henry defeated him at the Battle of Tinchebrai, in Normandy, in 1106. Robert was taken prisoner and kept in England until he died in 1134. On his tomb in Gloucester Cathedral, England, he is dressed as a soldier. One leg is crossed over the other to show that he had been on a crusade.

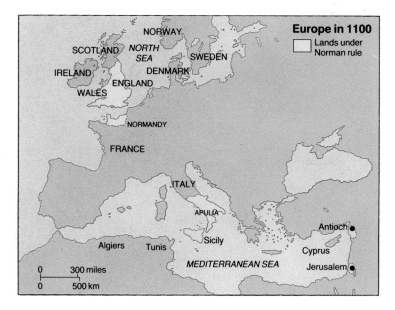

Europe in 1100

☐ Lands under Norman rule

NORWAY
SCOTLAND
NORTH SEA
SWEDEN
IRELAND
DENMARK
ENGLAND
WALES
NORMANDY
FRANCE
ITALY
APULIA
Antioch
Algiers
Tunis
Sicily
Cyprus
MEDITERRANEAN SEA
Jerusalem

0   300 miles
0   500 km

◁ **The Norman world.**

The Normans took part in the **Crusades** to the Holy Land from 1096 until the end of the twelfth century. For some of this time Crusaders occupied Jerusalem, Antioch and Tripoli. In 1147 Roger II of Sicily occupied a long stretch of the North African coast and in 1191 Richard I of England conquered Cyprus.

When Richard I died in 1199, his brother John became King of England. John was also Duke of Normandy, Anjou, Touraine and Maine, but by 1204 he had lost all his French territory to the King of France. He tried to win it back in 1214, but failed. John was the last king of England who was also Duke of Normandy. After his death the two places became quite separate and were never reunited.

The Normans and the English language
When the French-speaking Normans came to England, the English people took over many French words. Words like *royal, parliament, judge* and *tax* come from French, and show that the Normans were important rulers. The Normans also increased the importance of the Church, and gave words like *prayer, saint* and *miracle*. English words for types of meat, like *mutton* and *beef,* also come from French. But English words for the animals themselves, like *sheep* and *cow,* come from words that were used in England before the Normans arrived. This is because the Normans were rich and ate most of the meat, while English people looked after the animals.

◁ **Typical Norman carvings** around a door at Ely Cathedral in England. Norman craftsmen liked to decorate their buildings with arches like these around the doors and windows. They carved figures of people, animals and plants into the stone. Sometimes they carved a scene from the Bible on the panel above the door. This one shows Christ in heaven, being carried by angels.

Digging up the past

The Normans left behind them objects that now lie buried underground in the places where they lived – sometimes beneath modern towns and cities. A lot of what we know about the Normans comes from the work of **archaeologists**, people who dig at different sites to uncover these objects, or **artefacts**.

In the past many **excavations** took place at castles that were built in Norman times. As the ruins of many of these buildings could still be seen, archaeologists had no problems in knowing where to dig. They excavated at Caen in Normandy and at many sites in England, Italy, Sicily, Cyprus and Syria. On these sites they uncovered evidence that told them a lot about the rich people who had lived and fought there.

For a long time, however, archaeologists knew very little about the everyday lives of the ordinary people who lived in towns and villages. This was because many of the places where they lived had been destroyed and the Norman remains were buried underneath more recent buildings. Although some sites had been excavated when buildings in towns were demolished, archaeologists were often more interested in looking for Roman remains than

◁ **An excavation** at Milk Street in London. Underneath a more recent building, archaeologists have discovered the foundations of the undercroft, or cellar, of a twelfth century house. Most houses in towns were made of wood at this time so this one is quite unusual. It was probably the home of a wealthy merchant or craftsman, as poor people could not afford to have houses built of stone.

◁ **The ridge and furrow pattern of medieval ploughed fields** shows up well beneath present-day pastures. Snow fills the furrows and leaves the ridges standing out clearly. These markings still show today because these fields have not been ploughed since medieval times. When the climate turned colder and wetter, the crops could no longer grow in some places and the ploughed fields were given over to sheep pasture.

Norman ones. Over the last 30 years, however, archaeologists in Britain have led the way in excavating town sites from the Norman period. Because of this, more evidence about the lives of the Normans comes from England than from anywhere else where the Normans lived.

An archaeologist's work

Looking for artefacts is only a part of an archaeologist's work. To put together a complete picture of Norman life, all finds must be recorded. The information is often stored in a computer. Some objects, such as stone foundations for buildings, cannot be moved from the site. These are measured carefully and also drawn and photographed. Smaller finds – such as scraps of cloth, coins, pottery, tools and leather – are cleaned and preserved. Archaeologists also take samples of soil from the site. These soil samples are studied in a laboratory. They contain the remains of insects, animal bones and seeds. From these remains, archaeologists know what the Normans ate and what their living conditions were like.

△ **Bone skates** from the Moorfields area of London. In Norman times Moorfields was a moor or marsh which froze over in the winter. In the twelfth century a man called William Fitz Stephen described how young men tied the shin-bones of animals to their feet for skates and then used an iron-spiked pole to push themselves across the ice.

7

History in words and pictures

The pictures that the Normans painted and the words they wrote provide a lot of information about what they did and how they lived. Men such as William of Jumiéges and William of Poitiers wrote books about the life of William the Conqueror. Both these men lived in Normandy and spoke French, but their books were written in Latin. This was the language the Romans had used. In Norman times it was used for church services and so all priests and monks had to learn it. *The Anglo-Saxon Chronicle* tells of the main events in England all through the Norman period. In 1086 William the Conqueror ordered the Domesday Book which tells us who owned what land in England at that time.

Clues in pictures

Many of the monks living in Norman times spent their days making copies of the Bible and other religious books. These copies are illuminated manuscripts. They are beautifully decorated, often with little

▽ **A page from the Domesday Book.** At Christmas 1085 William the Conqueror decided he wanted to know more about England. He wanted to know 'how it was occupied – and with what sort of people'. To do this, he sent teams of men to every manor in the country. The men had to find out as much as possible about each manor. This included who it belonged to, how much it was worth, how many peasants lived there and how many plough teams there were. All this information was brought to Winchester. There it was written up by a scribe into the Domesday Books we can see here today. The word 'Domesday' means judgement. It was used to describe the books because no one was allowed to question what was written in them.

pictures in the first capital letter of each chapter. The pictures give us an idea about what life was like in those days. The scenes were often from the Bible, but the monks drew the people as if they were living in Norman times. Pictures on calendars show scenes from country life. They show us how people ploughed their fields and harvested their crops.

Churches were often decorated with scenes from the Bible as many people could not read. Some scenes were painted on the walls, but others were carved on little wooden seats called **misericords.** Stained glass windows often told a story, too. Some at Canterbury Cathedral in England show St Thomas à Becket bringing a dead boy back to life. The boy's parents promise to give money to the Church in thanks for this miracle.

The most famous pictures from Norman times are on the Bayeux Tapestry. This **tapestry** was probably made in Kent in England soon after William the Conqueror came to England. It tells the story of the Norman conquest of England from William's side and also shows us many details of everyday life in Normandy and England. It was made for the Bishop of Bayeux in Normandy. His name was Odo and he was half-brother to William the Conqueror.

△ **A scribe at work.** This picture is from a copy of St Mark's Gospel made in France in Norman times. At this time all books had to be copied out by hand. The pictures had to be painted by hand, too. This picture shows St Mark writing his Gospel. It also shows the lion which was the symbol for St Mark. At first all this work was done by monks, but later there were also professional writers called scribes. They all wrote with a quill pen made from a goose feather. This was kept sharp with a knife and dipped in red or black ink. There was no paper in Norman times so the scribes wrote on parchment which was made from animal skin.

◁ **Cooks preparing a banquet** for William the Conqueror. This scene is taken from the Bayeux Tapestry. The reason for making the tapestry was to tell the story of the conquest of England by the Normans, but scenes like this one can also tell us a lot about everyday life at that time.

How the Normans ruled their lands

The Normans believed all the land belonged to the king. When he gave land to his **barons**, they became his **vassals.** This meant they had to give him money in the form of taxes and help him to fight his enemies. If a baron displeased the king, however, the king could take his lands back. Because of this, the barons were said to 'hold' their land, rather than to 'own' it. This system of holding land in exchange for services is known as **feudalism.** William the Conqueror introduced it to England when he became king. He kept some land for himself and gave some to the Church. He gave the rest to the barons who came with him from Normandy. These barons were his tenants-in-chief and 1400 of them were listed in the Domesday Book. They did not all have the same amount of land, however, as just ten of them held a quarter of the land between them.

The barons gave land to the **knights** who had followed them from Normandy. In exchange, each knight gave 40 days' military service a year to his baron. He had to be armed and on horseback. He also had to bring a certain number of soldiers with him.

◁ **This picture shows William the Conqueror** on the left, holding a model of Battle Abbey. On the right is his son, William Rufus, with a model of Westminster Hall. Norman kings encouraged the building of new churches, cathedrals and abbeys like these ones, because the kings believed that their power came from God. The king would give the barons permission to build castles on the land they held from him. These castles were one way of reminding the people of the king's power. Only a few people would ever see the king in Norman times, but he made sure nobody forgot how important he was.

Military service was expensive for knights. To raise money each knight gave land to a number of **peasants**. They usually lived in villages and had to work for the knight who was lord of the manor. They also farmed some land for themselves.

Not everyone worked on the land. In towns, some people made their living from trading or making things to sell. They were called **burgesses** and often held their property direct from the king. If a peasant could run away and hide in a town for a year and a day, he was freed from his duties to his lord. He could also buy his freedom if he could earn the extra money he needed.

Law and order

The barons and knights, who held land from the king, also had the right to hold courts. Here they tried people for small crimes on their estates. These included fighting, cutting firewood without permission, and small-scale theft. The punishment for these crimes was usually a fine. People accused of murder and other serious crimes were tried in a county court by a **sheriff** who was appointed by the king. If someone was found guilty of murder, he might be blinded and have his hands chopped off. Prisons were only used for people who were waiting to be tried.

△ **The king's seal.** This seal belonged to William the Conqueror. He used it on letters and other documents to show that they came from the king. He was a clever soldier, but he could neither read nor write. Neither could many of his barons. Because of this, the seal meant the same as a signature on a letter or a document today. At first only the king had a seal, but by the end of the Norman period many knights and merchants had them, too.

◁ **The lord's reeve watching the villeins** to see that they do his work properly. Harvest was a busy time for everyone as the villeins wanted to cut their own crops at the same time as their lord wanted them to cut his. This picture shows the reeve carrying a horn to call the villeins to him and a stick to beat them if they disobey his orders.

Clothes and appearance

Norman homes were usually cold and draughty, no matter how rich the owners were. Norman people also spent much of their time outside. Because of this, they wore clothes to keep themselves warm, rather than to be stylish. Most of what we know about these clothes comes from pictures in Norman manuscripts and from carvings on gravestones. For example, a **baron** in the twelfth century was told to wear 'a fur-lined cloak, or mantle, a tunic with sleeves, stockings, laced boots or leather shoes, and an undershirt of silk or linen'. A young girl wore 'a **linen** undergarment, a white fur mantle, a silk gown, or kirtle, and embroidered stockings and shoes'.

The peasants wore very simple clothes. In summer men and boys wore long-sleeved tunics which came down almost to their knees. Their legs were usually bare and they often went without shoes. They usually wore a hood to protect them from the sun and the rain when they were working outside. In winter they also wore trousers which were held tightly to their legs below the knee by criss-crossed laces. They wore boots made of thick cloth or rough leather. When it was very cold, they also wore woollen cloaks or extra tunics without sleeves.

◁ **These twelfth century shoes** were found on two sites in London. The shoes are made out of leather and have a drawstring around the ankle to hold them onto the wearer's foot. The shoe on the right is decorated with an embroidered stripe down the front. Leather usually rots away in the ground and so finds like these are quite rare.

◁ **The clothing of wealthy women,** from a fourteenth century manuscript. This is a little later than the Norman period, but fashions changed so slowly that women in the twelfth century would also have worn clothes very much like these. They wore their hair in long plaits wound around their heads and many women hid their hair under a hat or a wimple. This was a head-dress made of two pieces of linen. One framed the face and the other covered the top of the head. Wimples were worn by poor women as well as by rich ones. No complete garments have been found from the Norman age and so we have to rely on pictures like this to tell us how people dressed at that time.

Women and girls also dressed simply. Their main garment was a long-sleeved dress, or kirtle, which reached down to their ankles. The kirtle was made of woollen cloth and was sometimes worn with a tie-belt or girdle around the waist. When they were not barefooted, women also wore shoes made of thick cloth or rough leather. In winter they kept warm by wearing woollen cloaks fastened at the neck with a brooch or a drawstring.

What archaeologists have found

At some excavations small scraps of woollen and linen cloth have been found. Their colours have faded, but archaeologists have analysed the chemicals in them and found that the Normans dyed their clothes using juice from plants called woad, madder and greenweed. These gave the colours blue, dark red and yellow. Archaeologists have also found traces of soap made from meat fat, wood ash and soda, which the Normans used to wash themselves in wooden bathtubs. Clothes were washed in rivers or streams. The women put a mixture of wood ash and clay on the clothes and beat them in the water with wooden paddles until they were clean.

△ **This brooch probably belonged to a rich French baron** or merchant. He would use it to fasten his cloak. Unlike their Viking ancestors, the Normans kept their wealth in land and so they never had much jewellery.

Family life

Children of rich Norman families spent the first part of their childhood at home, with tutors to give them lessons in reading and writing. When they were eight or nine, however, they were often sent away. The girls went to convents or to other castles where they learnt sewing, embroidery, cooking and good manners. The boys went away to start their training to become knights and to have lessons in Latin and French. In contrast, poor children stayed at home until they got married. They had no proper education. Instead they learned about farming by helping on the family land as soon as they could walk.

Getting married

If a rich man died and left young children, the king could take over his estates until the children **came of age**. The king could also choose marriage partners for the man's children. To avoid this, a girl from a rich family might be betrothed, or engaged, at the age of nine or ten to someone her father had chosen for her. She might be married before she was fourteen and at her wedding she received gifts from everyone on her

▽ **A Norman font** in the church of St Michael at Castle Frome in Herefordshire, England. Because many children died young, parents liked to have babies baptized soon after birth. The baptism took place at the local church in a font of holy water. At the church, salt was put into the baby's mouth. Its ears and nostrils were wetted with saliva. Oil was smeared on its back and breast, then it was dipped three times in the font. It went first on its right side, then on its left, and then face down in the water. Then it was lifted out by its chief godparent. The font in this picture was made around 1140. The carving is of a baptism and shows the hand of God, together with Christ and a dove.

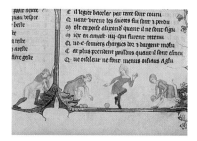

father's estates. She also took a **dowry** with her to her husband's family. This dowry was usually a sum of money, but it could also be property or land.

Married women

When a rich woman married, she usually spent a lot of time at home on her own while her husband went abroad or to the king's court. During this time she had to take his place and look after his household and his estates. To do this properly, many rich women made the effort to learn to read. They knew a lot about the world beyond their homes. A poor woman had no such chance of becoming educated. She could choose her own husband but being married usually led her into a life of great hardship. She had to help her husband in the fields, as well as cooking, making clothes and looking after the house. Few babies survived, so she might have a baby every year in the hope that one or two would live to be adults.

Hard times

In Norman times, people did not live as long as people do today. Life was hard. Sometimes there was not enough food for everyone and poor people starved. No one knew about keeping wounds clean and so even a healthy person might die as a result of a cut hand or foot. There was a lot of illness, but no one knew how it was caused. Many looked on it as a punishment from God and no cures were known.

△ **Some children's games in Norman times** were very much like the games we still play today. These pictures are from the border of an early fourteenth century manuscript. The first one shows a group of boys playing a game of bowls similar to a game played in Australia today. In this game one boy throws the ball at his opponent and aims to hit him below the knee. The second picture shows two boys whipping tops. The boys on the third picture are playing a game of chance using a dice board.

The Church

Every Norman village had its own church and towns usually had more than one. It was difficult for people to forget the power of the Church, and it played an important part in their lives, even though not everyone was very religious. William the Conqueror was a devout Christian, however, and so were many of his followers. After he became King of England, he gave over a quarter of the land there to the Church. This made the Church very wealthy.

Bishops and priests

Each church was the centre of a **parish** in which about 250 people lived. The parishes were grouped together into **dioceses** and at the head of each diocese was a bishop.

William replaced the English bishops with men from Normandy. These Norman bishops were William's **vassals**, but their positions as church leaders made them powerful men. A bishop was always a well educated man and had usually studied at one of the big monasteries in Normandy.

Although bishops were well-educated, the parish priest was often not much better educated than the people in his parish. He could say Mass, baptize babies and bury the dead. However, some priests could not even read or write and so they learnt the services by heart. As the services were all in Latin, no one in the village would know if he made a mistake.

Holy days and holidays

For the Normans there were no holidays as we know them. People had to look after the farmland all year round. Sunday was a day of rest, however, and often Monday was too. Not much work could be done in winter and so Christmas celebrations lasted for 12 days after Christmas Day. People collected eggs during Lent and boiled them in coloured water on

△ **The church at the Abbaye aux Dames at Caen** in Normandy. This was founded by William the Conqueror, who also founded the Abbaye aux Hommes in the same town. Because religion played a very important part in Norman life, the church was usually one of the largest buildings in a town or a village. The churches were built of stone and many of them were richly decorated with rounded arches over the windows and doors. The towers were usually square and also decorated with arches. Sometimes spires were added at a later date.

Good Friday. The priest blessed the eggs and then people ate them as part of the Easter Sunday celebrations. Other Holy Days were Whitsuntide, Michaelmas and feast days of the Virgin Mary. The Normans also celebrated many Saints' Days throughout the year with colourful processions around the village and everyone stopped work to watch.

△ **A stained glass window with a scene from the Bible.** This window is in Canterbury Cathedral and shows the Holy Family on their Flight into Egypt to escape from Herod. Windows like this were very popular in Norman times. Their rich colours brightened up the church. The pictures in the windows helped people to remember the stories from the Bible at a time when very few people could read.

Holy journeys

A pilgrimage was a journey to a holy place such as Jerusalem, or to a shrine where the remains of the body of a saint, or relics, were kept. These journeys were important to the Normans and people had many reasons for going on them.

Some pilgrims went because they had done something wrong and wanted to be forgiven. Others went because they were very religious and some went just to enjoy themselves. People called palmers were paid to go on pilgrimages in place of people who could not go themselves.

Most pilgrims were looking for medical help, however. They thought that looking at the relics of saints would cure their illnesses. They always left money at the shrine. This meant that a church with relics could become very rich. Soon people began selling fake relics. They tricked other people into paying large sums of money to see the Devil's tail or Christ's breath in a jar.

◁ **Pilgrims used to buy lead badges** like these ones to remind them of a particular pilgrimage. Each shrine had a badge with a different design. These three are all from English shrines. From left to right they are St Thomas à Becket at Canterbury, Edward the Confessor in London, and Our Lady of Walsingham in Norfolk.

Monasteries and convents

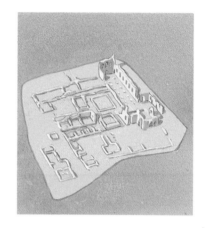

S ome of the greatest Norman buildings that we can still see today are the monasteries. Two of the most famous were Bec and Jumièges in Normandy. These were centres of learning, as well as religious centres. Many priests and bishops trained there. When William the Conqueror arrived in England, he thought that God had helped him win the Battle of Hastings. To show how grateful he was, he decided to rebuild the English monasteries and to found some new ones. William invited monks from Normandy to help him and by the year 1200 England had over 300 monasteries and convents.

Monks and nuns

People had different reasons for joining monasteries or convents. Some men went to train to be priests and only stayed a few years. Others spent their whole lives there. Some rich women went because they were very religious. Others became nuns because they did not want to marry the men their fathers had chosen for them. Monks and nuns were sometimes given the task of educating young boys and girls, but this happened more often in Normandy than in England. Poor people also went to live in monasteries and convents. They became lay-brothers and lay-sisters who did the jobs and looked after the sheep. In exchange, they had three meals a day and their own range of buildings to live in. Many found this better than trying to make a living in a village.

Monks and nuns promised to give up riches and were supposed to live a simple life of prayer and meditation. At first they did this, but soon rich men started to make gifts of land and money to the monasteries. They did not give their best farmland, however. Instead, they gave moorland and rough pasture. The monks kept sheep on this. They sold the wool for profit and the monasteries became rich.

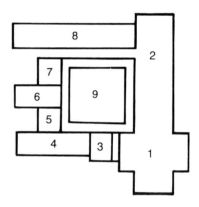

△ **The ruins of Byland Abbey** in Yorkshire, England. The diagram shows how the abbey was laid out and the names of the different rooms.

1 Monks' choir
2 Lay brothers' choir
3 Chapter house
4 Dormitory
5 Warming house
6 Refectory
7 Kitchen
8 Lay brothers' range
9 Cloister

A day in a monastery

At Hexham Abbey a monk's day started at two o'clock in the morning with a service, or office, called Matins. This was held in the choir of the church and was soon followed by another office, called Lauds, then the monks went back to bed in the dormitory. The monks got up at sunrise for the office called Prime, then spent an hour reading before breakfast. After breakfast came the office of Tierce, followed by Mass. After that they sometimes went to the chapter house to discuss the day's business. They worked until midday, then went into church for the office called Sext. This was followed by High Mass and the office of None, then they went to the refectory, for dinner. They worked again until evening prayers, or Vespers, which were said at four o'clock in winter and six o'clock in summer. Then they had supper before the last office of the day which was called Compline. After that they went to bed – until two o'clock when the daily round of offices started again.

△ **The warming chamber at Lacock Abbey** in Wiltshire, England. Monks were allowed to come in here for short periods when the weather was very cold. However, older monks and those who had been ill were allowed to stay in the warming chamber a little longer.

◁ **A monk teaching other monks.** This picture also shows us the sort of clothes that the monks wore. Each had a long woollen robe, called a habit. It had a hood which the monk pulled over his head in cold weather. This hood was needed because of the monk's hairstyle. The hairstyle was called a tonsure and meant that the hair on the top of his head was shaved off.

Living on the land

The peasants who farmed the land often lived in villages. They were divided into groups according to how much land they held. The biggest group were known as **villeins**. Each villein farmed around 12 hectares. This land was in the open fields which surrounded the village. There were usually two or three fields, each divided into **strips.** If a villein had 30 strips of land, he would have an equal number in each field. However, his strips were scattered across the field so that each villein got a mixture of good and poor soil.

Working for the lord of the manor

The village belonged to the lord of the manor and the villeins had to spend two or three days each week farming some of the strips for the lord. They also had to work on the lord's own manor farm, or **demesne.** At hay-time and harvest they had to do extra work, called boon-work, for the lord of the manor. Each year the villeins had to give him some of the produce of their land, or else a sum of money. They also had to give one-tenth of their produce to the Church.

Below the villeins were people called **cottars** or **bordars.** They farmed about two hectares of land

The village blacksmith
The blacksmith was one of the craftsmen you would find in every Norman village. He melted iron in his forge and then hammered it into shape on his **anvil.** As well as making horse-shoes, he also made tools and mended them when they were broken. Many people believed the blacksmith was also some kind of witch-doctor. He made small metal figures called charms which people believed had magic powers to cure their toothaches and headaches. They thought he could also stop wounds from bleeding.

◁ **A blacksmith working at his forge,** melting iron to make into tools.

each and had to work for the lord for at least one day a week. Beneath them were the **serfs** who had no land and spent most of the time working for the lord of the manor. In return he gave them food and somewhere to live. They had no control over what happened to them. The lord of the manor was even allowed to sell them.

The rest of the people were **freemen** or sokemen. They owned their own land and had no master except the king. They could sell their land and live somewhere else if they wanted to. They could also sell their produce and keep the profit.

This kind of **feudal system** was found mainly in the parts of England where grain crops like wheat and barley grew easily. It was also found in Normandy as many of the rich barons held land in both countries. In other areas, however, people lived on scattered farms rather than in compact villages and so the feudal system could not be made to work.

▽ **A typical Norman village** had a church, a manor house and a mill, and perhaps an orchard. There were few hedges or walls, but a deep lane separated the fields from the cottage gardens. The houses were built from wood and mud and thatched with straw. The mud floor of the single room was covered in straw and there was a hearth in the middle. There was a hole in the roof, but most of the smoke stayed inside. The windows had wooden shutters but no glass and there was a leather curtain instead of a door. The room was very draughty. There was little furniture, apart from a cooking pot and perhaps a bench. The family shared its home with the pigs and hens.

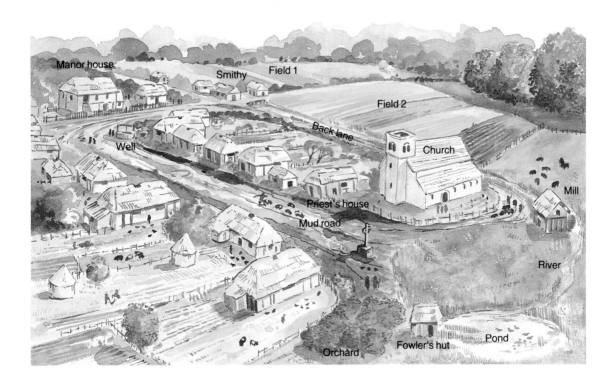

Manor house · Smithy · Field 1 · Field 2 · Back lane · Well · Church · Mill · Priest's house · Mud road · River · Fowler's hut · Pond · Orchard

Where food came from

A Norman **villein** hardly ever went outside the village where he lived. There were two reasons for this. One was that he was not allowed to leave the village without his lord's permission. The other was that he could find almost everything he needed in and around the village itself. As well as his 30 strips of land on which he grew wheat, oats, barley or rye, he had a garden behind his house. There his wife grew vegetables such as peas, beans and onions. She also grew herbs such as parsley, sage and mint. There would probably be an apple tree, a pear tree and a quince bush.

Hens and chickens scratched around the garden in the day and were brought into the house at night to protect them from foxes. Bees were kept in hives which looked like large wicker baskets. People collected honey from the beehives and used it to sweeten food and drink as there was no sugar. They also collected wax from the honeycombs and made it into candles. Some villagers might keep a pig or two in the garden, but in the autumn they would send the pigs to a nearby wood to feed on acorns. The villeins could also go into this wood to gather firewood from trees that had fallen over or blown down. In the autumn they could gather wild nuts and berries.

▽ **Ploughing a field in January.** The plough is heavy as parts of it are made from iron and it needs four oxen to pull it. Some ploughs needed six or more oxen. The oxen needed a lot of space to turn around and this might be one reason why a lot of fields at this time did not have hedges or walls to mark their boundaries. This way of farming is called 'the open field system'. The picture comes from a calendar from the 11th century. Calendars like these tell us a lot of what we know about the farmer's year in Norman times.

A villein was allowed to use the **common land** in the village, as well as his share of the fields and the hay meadow. He could tether his goats, which he kept for their milk, on the common land. If he was lucky enough to have a cow, that could graze there too, and so could his sheep.

Making the most of the land

Each year one field was also left open for animals to graze on. This was because the villeins had realized that if they grew the same crop in a field every year, the soil became poor and the crop failed to grow properly. To avoid this, they only used two of the three fields at a time and changed the crops so that no field grew the same for two years running. This was called crop rotation and, to make it work well, the third field had to be left empty or fallow for a year. When the animals grazed on it, their manure helped to put goodness back into the soil.

Many animals were killed for meat at the beginning of winter. However, sheep were kept for their wool and their milk until they were about seven years old. By that time their meat was quite tough and the villein's wife had to boil it for a long time.

△ **Sowing seed.** The Bayeux Tapestry shows us scenes of everyday life in England and in Normandy. Most of these are along the top and bottom borders of the tapestry. This picture shows poor people preparing their land in spring. After the fields were ploughed, the seed for the next crop was planted. This was done by a man who walked along and scattered the seed to either side from a bag round his neck. This was called broadcast sowing. A harrow was then pulled over the seeded area to cover it with soil. Wild birds liked to eat the seed at this point and so the village children went to the fields to chase them off.

▽ **Catching rabbits.** One woman sends a ferret into the rabbit warren to chase the rabbits, while her friend holds a net to trap the rabbits as they run out. The Normans introduced rabbits to England so that the lord of the manor could eat meat in winter. The rabbits lived in warrens and a man called a warrener looked after them. But sometimes peasants tried to steal one for their own cooking-pot.

The manor house

The lord of the manor was in a middle position in Norman society, more powerful than the **villeins** but not as powerful as the **barons.** He was usually a knight and he held his land from a baron. The baron would have many **manors** and would live in a castle a long way away from most of them. The lord of the manor, however, lived in the same village as the villeins and **cottars** who farmed his land for him. His house was usually separated from the rest of the village by some of its **demesne** lands. It was bigger than the other houses and more strongly built. It was also surrounded by a fenced courtyard in which

▽ **Boothby Pagnall Hall,** a manor house in Lincolnshire, England was built around the year 1200. The walls and the roof are all made of stone. The only way you could reach the main hall, which was the living area, was through the door at the top of the staircase on the left. At one end of the hall was the solar, or private room, for the lord of the manor and his family. At ground level were cellars where food and wine could be stored.

stood the stables, the storerooms and the dairy. Archaeologists have noticed that if the manor house was built of wood, the kitchen was also in the courtyard. This was to make sure that if a fire started while food was being cooked, it would not spread to the rest of the manor house.

Inside the manor house

The great hall of the manor house was where most of the daily activities took place. At different times of day it had to be a dining room, a court room, and a bedroom for the servants. The hunting dogs and hawks probably lived in there as well. The floor was covered with herbs and rushes which were brought by the villeins' wives. These women also had to make the **rushlights** – candles made of rushes – and beeswax candles to light the manor house at night. The manor had its own carpenter who made the furniture. There would be a table and perhaps carved chairs for the lord of the manor and his wife and any important guests. There would also be a few wooden chests and cupboards in which clothes could be kept. The servants used benches around the great hall as seats by day and beds by night. The hall was open to the wooden rafters and it was built as high as possible so that sparks from the fire did not set the roof alight.

△ **The hall of the manor house at Stokesay Castle** in Shropshire, England. This was the most important room in the manor house and all the day's activities went on there. At Stokesay the hall was on the second floor of the house and the only way into it was by an outside staircase leading up from the courtyard. The staircase in this picture leads up to the lord of the manor's private room, or solar.

◁ **The furniture in a Norman manor house** was usually plain and practical, like this wooden chest. Not much of it has survived. One reason for this is that there never was very much furniture in a manor house anyway. Another reason is that old furniture was chopped up and burned as firewood when it was no longer needed.

The castle-builders

We can still see the ruins of many Norman castles today, in England, Italy and the Holy Land as well as in Normandy itself. These castles were built by the **barons.** They built castles on their lands to remind people how important they were.

A castle was also a place where the baron and his followers could defend themselves from their enemies. Sometimes they had to do this quickly and did not have time to build a stone castle. Instead they used earth and wood to build what was called a **motte-and-bailey** castle. The people who lived on the baron's estate were forced to help with the building. **Archaeologists** have found that while some people dug a moat around the bailey, others built a tall wooden tower. The earth from the moat was then piled up around the bottom of the tower to make a mound or a motte. These castles could be completed in two to three weeks.

▽ **A motte-and-bailey castle.** Inside the bailey were houses, stables, storerooms and workshops and it was there that the people of the castle lived most of the time. If an enemy attacked, however, the people of the castle hurried up the steps of the motte and into the tower at the top. If they had enough food and water stored there, they could stay in the tower until the enemy was defeated and went away. No motte-and-bailey castles can be seen today, because wood rots quickly. But many of the mounds and moats still exist, and archaeologists have excavated some of them. The evidence that they found gives us an idea of what these early castles looked like.

◁ **The keep was the strongest part of the castle.** People could go there for safety when the castle was attacked. This picture shows the remains of the keep at Barnard Castle, in England. One of the arrow slits can be seen in the wall on the right. The Normans usually built their castles on sites which were easy to defend against any enemies who tried to attack them. Barnard Castle is at the top of a sheer cliff overlooking the River Tees.

△ **Builders' tools and methods of working** are clearly shown in this picture from a Norman manuscript. They had no machines to help them and so they had to do everything by hand. Sometimes they used a rope and a pulley wheel to help them to lift baskets full of bricks or stones to where they were needed. In this picture, however, the men are lifting the basket up without any help at all.

Stone fortresses

Stone castles took much longer to build. First an architect or master **mason** was chosen to design the castle. Often he came from France and so did his chief assistants. They received high wages for their work, but the baron or his steward forced the local men into helping the masons without being paid. Tools in those days were simple, and so the work was hard and many men were needed. For example, over 1600 men were needed to build Beaumaris Castle, in Wales. Some of these were employed on breaking up poor quality stone and flint. This was mixed with cement and heavy chains and poured inside the thick walls of the castle. When it set, it was as hard as any rock and cost a lot less money than if the walls had been built of solid stone. Many castle walls were built this way.

Living in a castle

The baron and his household got up early every morning and went to Mass in the castle chapel. Then they had breakfast, before starting on the day's work. For the baron this meant going into the great hall of the castle with the steward who looked after his estates. They sat on a raised platform, or dais, and talked about estate matters. They also solved problems for tenants who came to visit them. This kept them busy until ten or eleven o'clock when they ate the main meal of the day. If there were no more estate matters to deal with, the baron probably spent the afternoon hunting or hawking. When he came back to the castle, he might take a bath, sitting on a stool in a wooden tub. He then changed his clothes and went back into the hall for supper.

The baron's wife would spend the day with the other ladies in the castle. They would do some embroidery or **tapestry**, and perhaps make up stories and riddles. The children only joined their mother when lessons were over.

After supper there might be some entertainment in the hall. Perhaps musicians or acrobats would perform by the light of candles and **rushlights.** When the entertainment was over, the captain of the guard made sure that all the sentries were at their posts. Then the baron and his wife went to bed.

Servants and retainers

The baron employed a second steward whose job was to keep life running smoothly inside the castle. The most important servants, called retainers, were the chamberlain who looked after the great hall, the cook, the butcher, the baker, the pantler in the pantry and the butler in the wine cellar. They had teams of servants to help them, and so did the keeper of the wardrobe who made sure the baron and his family had clothes to wear.

△ **The great hall in the keep of Castle Hedingham** in Essex, England, would not have looked so neat and tidy in Norman times. All meals were eaten in there and, apart from the baron and his wife, everyone slept in there at night. Some slept on straw-filled mattresses on benches along the walls, but others slept on the floor. It was covered with herbs and rushes, but these soon got greasy from spilled food and candle-fat. The windows had no glass and the fireplace in the wall did not have a proper flue. This meant that smoke came back into the room and blew about in the draughts. It soon darkened the whitewashed walls and spoiled any tapestries which were hanging there.

Children in the castle

The baron's children spent most of their day away from their parents. Young children were usually looked after by nurses. Older children spent the morning and early afternoon with their tutors and then joined their mother. In fine weather they played games in the courtyard. After supper they sometimes watched the entertainments. Because people in Norman times did not expect to live to be very old, childhood was short. By the age of 10, the baron's children were thought to be old enough to leave home. The boys went to the households of other barons where they trained to be knights. The girls went to convents to be educated.

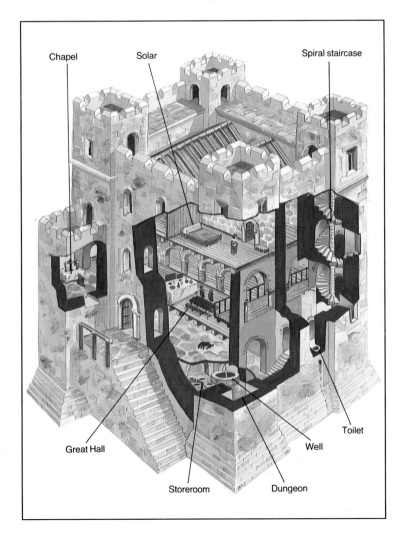

Chapel   Solar   Spiral staircase

Great Hall

Storeroom   Dungeon

Well   Toilet

◁ **Inside the keep.** The earliest keeps were square like this one, but later ones were round as this shape was easier to defend from enemies. The great hall and chapel were on the second floor, with cellars and storerooms underneath. On the ground floor there was also a well. This meant that if the castle was besieged, the people inside had a supply of water as well as food. Toilets were built into the thickness of the wall. If they were well planned, they drained into a river or a stream. Otherwise a servant had to empty them as needed. The lord's solar was above the great hall. It was reached by the spiral staircases up the inside of the four corner towers. Sentries standing on the tops of the towers could see who was approaching the castle. The keep was usually in an inner bailey which had the kitchen, the granary and more storerooms surrounded by a wall. Outside this wall was the outer bailey, which had the stables, a garden and an exercise yard for the horses.

Towns and cities

Norman towns were much smaller than towns today. Unlike today's cities with millions of people, some Norman towns had as few as 500 people living in them and even important centres like York and Norwich had fewer than 10 000. London, which was one of Europe's biggest cities, only had 20 000 people by the end of the twelfth century.

In the last 30 years **archaeologists** have been able to excavate many sites in towns that date back to Norman times. Most of these have been in England, but parts of William the Conqueror's city of Caen in Normandy have also been excavated. Big excavations in England have been at Winchester and at King's Lynn. Documents written 900 years ago describe King's Lynn as it was when it was founded. Aerial photographs can give us an idea of how the streets and buildings were arranged.

Creating a new town

Many English towns were founded before the Normans arrived. However, the Normans realized that new towns were a way of making money. For example, if a baron had a town on his land, he could ask the king to give him the right to hold a market there. Once he got a market, he could persuade craftsmen and merchants to settle in the town. He would lay out streets and offer building plots, known

▽ **A water carrier bringing water into a town.** He probably got this water from a well and so it would be clean. In many towns, however, people got their water from a river or a stream. This water was used for drinking and cooking and washing. Sometimes it was also used in industries such as cloth-making, metal-working and tanning leather. There were no sewers or drains as we know them and so dirty water often went back into the river or stream that people used for drinking. Nobody knew that this dirty water could be a source of many diseases and so nobody tried to keep it clean. The streets were usually dirty, too. They were often unpaved and full of rotting rubbish.

◁ **Chipping Campden** became a borough in the late twelfth century. Chipping is an old English word for market and in Chipping Campden the market was held in the main street. The market place was boat-shaped and can be seen in the middle of the picture, though newer buildings now cover some of it. To either side of the main street the outlines of the burgage plots can be seen. These backed on to another street which separated the town from the fields. The houses were built at the front of the burgage plots, facing on to the main street.

as burgage plots, to people in exchange for rent.

Most people who lived in towns were **burgesses.** This meant that they had no **feudal** duties to do. They still had to obey the baron's laws, however. To avoid doing this, they could get together and buy a charter from the baron or from the king. They paid a yearly rent for this. In exchange, they could collect the market tolls, hold courts, elect magistrates, a **mayor** and **bailiffs,** and form **guilds** of merchants and craftsmen.

Like the villages, most towns were surrounded by open fields which were divided into **strips.** Some people went to work on these every day. As well as the fields, there was **common land** where the cattle and sheep grazed.

Many towns were also surrounded by a wall with gates to allow people in and out. At first the wall was there to defend the town from any attackers, including wild animals. Later it was used as a way of checking who came into the town.

△ **The house of Aaron the Jew** in Lincoln, England, has survived from Norman times because it was built of stone. Most Norman houses were built of wood which rotted or burnt down. The thatched roofs of most houses made fires a big problem as towns grew larger.

Craftworkers

Many craftsmen and merchants taught their skills to their sons and so kept their trade within their own families. Others employed **apprentices** to learn their trade. A boy could become an apprentice when he was about 11 or 12 years old. He was given his food and a place to live with the family of his master. He was also given a small amount of pocket money. In return, he had to do jobs such as sweeping up and fetching firewood, as well as learning his trade.

A boy was usually an apprentice for about six or seven years, though he could stay an apprentice for longer if that was what his master wanted. When his master thought the boy was good enough, he became a journeyman. This meant he could work for other men in his trade and earn more money. After a few years as a journeyman, he would probably earn enough money to start his own business. He then became a master and employed apprentices of his own.

△ **A woman weaves cloth on a loom.** The woman's feet rest on a treadle. When she pushes this down, ropes and pulleys lift up every second thread on the loom. She then throws a shuttle with another thread across between them. To keep the cloth firm, she pushes the thread from the shuttle into place with the smooth stick in her left hand. Then she pushes the treadle down again and throws the shuttle across the other way until the cloth is the length she wants.

◁ **A Norman potter** used a potter's wheel to make jugs and storage jars like these. He started by putting a lump of clay in the middle of his potter's wheel. Then he used a long stick to turn the wheel with one hand while he shaped the clay with the other. When the pot was the shape he wanted, he either painted it or scratched a simple pattern into the wet clay. After that the pot was baked in an oven over a kiln until it was hard.

Two craftworkers

The craftspeople you would find in a Norman town included carpenters, metalworkers and weavers. We know about the things they made and the way they made them from archaeological evidence and from pictures like these which are from Norman times.

◁ **This carpenter** is using tools which are not very different from the tools we use today. On his workbench he has a hammer, files and chisels. He would use these to make simple furniture or perhaps to carve a picture on a misericord like this one.

▽ **These metalworkers** are hammering pieces of metal into tools. The metal has been heated in the fire so that it will bend more easily and the men wear leather aprons to protect themselves from flying sparks. They also wear stout leather boots to protect their feet from pieces of sharp metal on the floor, but their legs are bare.

The guilds

Early on in Norman times, any man could set up a business if he had enough money. He could call himself a craftsman without working as an apprentice first. He could decide how much to pay his workers and also what price to charge for his goods. Other craftsmen who had served a long apprenticeship did not like this. They got together and formed **guilds**, groups of traders who together were powerful. Only craftsmen who had served an apprenticeship and charged fair prices could be members of guilds and it became difficult to find work if you were not a member. At first all the traders in the town were in one guild. As towns grew larger, each trade began to have its own guild of skilled men. The guilds fixed wages and prices and punished cheats. They had strict rules on who could be members. They also helped members who were sick and gave money to the widows and orphans of members who had died.

Markets and fairs

Once a week, people in a Norman town would buy what they needed at a market. At first these markets were in the churchyard on a Sunday. The merchants spread their goods out on the church wall and people came to buy them. Later a law was passed to forbid this, so merchants set up wooden market stalls in the streets of the town. In many towns a special market place was made. Because so many people would walk on the market place, it was often cobbled with smooth pebbles from a nearby river. Craftsmen liked to have their houses near the market place. This was because many of them used the front room of the house as a shop. There was no glass in the window, so the craftsmen could set up a shelf on the windowsill to display their goods.

On market day people from the nearby countryside came to town with produce such as eggs, cabbages and onions to sell on stalls in the market. They might also bring one or two of their animals to sell. If they were **freemen,** they had to pay a **toll** to get in to the town to sell their goods. If they were **villeins, cottars** or **bordars,** they also had to pay a fee to the lord of the manor for permission to leave their village.

Merchants and craftsmen did not have to pay any tolls in their home towns. If they went to sell their goods in another town, however, they would have to pay the toll to trade there. The main items they sold were pottery, metal goods such as pans and knives and leather goods like shoes, boots and belts.

Some people went to the market simply to enjoy a day out. They watched the street entertainers and ate hot pies from the baker's shop. The alehouses sold beer all day long and records from the local courts tell us that many men and women got drunk. Some of them also fought in the street. If they were caught, they were fined at the next meeting of the court.

△ **The market place** at Swaffham in Norfolk, England, was first laid out in Norman times and is still used for the market today. Just as traders do now, traders in Norman times set up their stalls in the open air. Some Norman markets were held around a stone cross. This showed traders and their customers that they were safe from robbers and outlaws while they were selling and buying. Other Norman towns had market halls. Some of these were built on two levels. From upstairs the market officers looked out to make sure trading was fair. Poor people who could not afford a stall of their own sold their goods in the open space at street level.

Fairs

Most towns had a fair once a year on the local saint's day. It was like the market, but much bigger. Traders came from further away and brought luxury goods such as linen and brassware. On a fair day, members of the local guilds might perform the Miracle plays. These were based on stories from the Bible or the lives of saints.

However much people were enjoying themselves, the Normans had a rule that everyone must be home by dark. At sunset the curfew bell rang and the town gates were shut to keep out unwelcome visitors and wild animals such as wolves. When they heard the curfew bell people had to put out their fires and were not allowed to light them again until morning. This was done to prevent sparks escaping during the night and setting the wooden houses on fire while the occupants were asleep. A nightwatchman then went round the streets, watching for fires, thieves and people breaking the curfew.

△ **Silver pennies made in the reign of William the Conqueror.** When the Dukes of Normandy became kings of England, they could have their own coins made. During William's reign, coins were made in about 70 different towns. The silver penny was the smallest one. Sometimes it was cut into two or four pieces to pay very small amounts. Not everyone paid for goods with money. Sometimes they paid by giving the seller some of their own goods in exchange for the item they wanted. This system was known as bartering. It was very popular with people in the country who never had much money of their own.

◁ **Performing bears** were very popular at fairs and markets. People could also enjoy watching wrestlers, jugglers and acrobats. There might be a wandering minstrel to sing songs and play music, and a jester who told jokes, played the fool and made people laugh.

Trading with the world

By the middle of the eleventh century life for most people in Europe was more peaceful than it had been since Roman times. The Viking raids of earlier centuries had ended and it was safe to build towns near the coast. But the Vikings had done good as well as harm, as they made links with traders from as far away as China and Baghdad. These links went on into Norman times. **Archaeologists** have found the remains of the luxury goods which traders bought and sold at international fairs. These include expensive materials like silk and brocade, and also little boxes and candlesticks made of brass.

Recipes tell us that spices such as pepper and ginger were brought from Asia and used by rich people to hide the taste of salted meat in winter. All of these things were luxury items that only the rich could afford. Most people still got their everyday needs from the village or town where they lived. Recipes also include raisins, almonds, dates, lemons and oranges, which you would not find in England or Normandy before Norman times. Norman knights first discovered these during the **Crusades** in the Holy Land, and brought them back to England and Normandy. We know that Normans ate these fruits because archaeologists have found some of the fruit-seeds in excavations.

Trading in Europe

The main trade routes, however, were between Normandy, England and the Low Countries, the region that today makes up Holland and Belgium. French wine was the best in Europe, so Normans who lived in England imported large quantities of it. The wine was shipped across the English Channel in wooden casks or in big earthenware jugs. Because all the **villeins** had to give the lord of the manor some of the produce from their land, he often had more than

△ **The different forms of transport** that the Normans used appear in these scenes from the Bayeux Tapestry. If the Normans had heavy loads to take over land, they used carts and wagons. These could be pulled by horses or oxen, though the one shown here is pulled by a man. Rich merchants with small amounts of goods could carry them on horseback. Poorer men had to walk. Travel over land was very slow and often uncomfortable. Because of this, the Normans used ships as much as possible. For journeys around the coast and across the sea, they used wooden ships with sails and oars. Smaller boats could sail on rivers and lakes and take goods inland. This meant that small ports could be built a long way from the sea.

he needed. He could sell some of the extra grain to people who needed it in other parts of the country. He also exported grain to Normandy, along with any extra honey and hides.

The most important export from the Norman lands was wool. It came from the **manors** and monasteries of England and Normandy and was sent to the Low Countries. There it was spun and woven into fine cloth which was sold at international fairs all over Europe.

Trading was still not completely safe, though, and not all goods reached their markets. Although there were few pirates, storms wrecked many ships at sea or blew them off course. Other ships sank in rivers before they even reached the coast.

▽ **Trade routes in Norman times.**

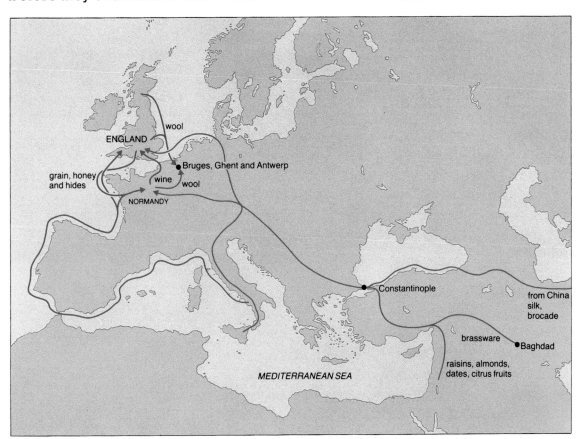

Cooking and eating

Manuscripts from Norman times often show
pictures of people eating. The manuscripts also
describe meals and recipes. Archaeologists have
found cooking pots, mugs and jugs. In the earthen
floors of excavated Norman buildings they have
found the remains of seeds and bones. The remains
have been studied carefully to find out where they
came from. All this evidence helps to put together a
good picture of what food the Normans ate and how
they cooked it. We also know how often the Normans
ate, and the differences between what the rich ate
and what the poor ate.

A poor person's daily meals

A **villein** and his family ate three meals a day. The
first was just a piece of barley bread and a cup of
water before they started work. The next meal was at
midday when the men came back from the fields.
This time they had barley bread and cheese and
drank either a cup of beer or a cup of cider. The main
meal was in the evening when work had finished for
the day. At this meal they drank beer or cider again.
They also had a bowl of soup, made with peas or
beans. Then they had salted pork or bacon, or
perhaps mutton stew if one of the old sheep had just
been killed. The stew was flavoured with herbs from
the garden and leeks and onions were sometimes
added to it.

The lord of the manor's diet

The lord of the manor ate his meals at around the
same time as the villeins. His food was better and
more interesting than theirs, however. His bread was
made from fine wheat flour and he had butter as well
as cheese. He drank wine instead of beer and ate
meat at midday, as well as in the evening. He could
afford to buy spices from abroad to hide the taste of

△ **A bronze cooking pot** like
this would have been used for
cooking at the manor house or
the castle. It had legs so that it
could be placed over the fire
without any other support.
Food was lifted out of it with a
three-pronged fork. The
villeins would also have a metal
cooking pot, but theirs would
be much smaller. Pictures in
manuscripts show us that these
cooking pots were also used as
baby-baths.

◁ **Food being prepared** for the lord of the manor or the baron in his castle. One man is probably stewing meat in the large cooking pots over the fire. This is done out of doors in case the flames get out of control. The man on the right is grinding meat into a paste which was then spread on bread and eaten. In the villeins' cottages the women cooked their stews and soups over the open hearth in the middle of the room. They sometimes also baked their bread on the hearth. The lord of the manor could fine the villeins for this if he found out, however. This was because he provided a bakehouse in the village and everyone had to pay to have their bread baked there.

▽ **A baker's shop at an army camp.** This shop probably just sold loaves of bread, like the ones on the counter. The Normans liked pastries and sweet things, however, and a baker's shop in a town would sell pies and tarts as well as bread.

salted meat in winter and ate beef, as well as pork, bacon and mutton. His evening meal finished with plum tart or apple flan, or even with raisins, dates and almonds which the **Crusaders** brought back from their travels.

Both rich and poor ate fish instead of meat on Fridays and for the 40 days of Lent. This was because the Church forbade them to eat meat at these times, in memory of Jesus' 40 days in the wilderness, and his death on Good Friday. Another reason for eating fish during Lent was that there was usually a shortage of fresh meat at this time of year. To provide this fish each manor had a fishpond, or **stew**. Fish were also caught in the rivers and brought in from the sea.

A Norman feast

If you were a guest at a Norman feast, you would have to bring your own knives and spoons. There were no forks and so everyone used their fingers to pick food up. The table for the lord and his family and their main guests was set up on a dais at one end of the great hall. The other tables were set at right angles to this with the next most important guests nearest the dais. On the lord's table there might be some **pewter** dishes. Everyone else used wooden **trenchers** or bowls. Often a piece of day-old bread was put in the bottom of the bowl and the soup was poured on top. If this bread was not eaten by the guests, it was later given to the poor who came to the castle to beg. Day-old bread was also sometimes used instead of a plate for eating slices of meat.

The feast often started with a fish course. This might be eels or herrings brought in from the coast or it might be freshwater fish from the castle's own fish **stew.** The fish was followed by several kinds of meat, perhaps beef and pork, and also wild birds such as pheasants and herons. Sometimes the meat was roasted on a **spit** and served in slices. At other times it was ground into a paste and mixed with milk, herbs and breadcrumbs, rather like a hamburger. Delicacies included larks' tongue pie and roasted peacock. There were rarely any vegetables served at a feast as they were thought to be 'peasants' food'.

▽ **A banquet scene** from the Bayeux Tapestry. On the left of the picture servants are bringing cooked chickens on spits from the kitchen. The men at the table in the middle are preparing the food for the guests — and one is sneaking a drink out of a drinking horn. At the table on the right, the guests are eating a fish course. There is also bread and cheese on the table. Feasts were held on special occasions, such as when the king visited the castle. They were also held at Christmas, when for one day the least important servant became the 'Lord of Misrule', changed places with the baron and sat at the high table.

◁ **Cutlery and crockery.** This picture of a medieval feast is taken from the Luttrell Psalter. This manuscript was written a little after Norman times, but the cutlery and crockery on the table would have been just the same. Some of the serving plates and bowls are made of a metal called pewter, which is a mixture of lead and tin. Others are made of pot and some are made of wood. There are not enough serving dishes for all the food, however, and some of the bread is placed straight onto the table.

After the meat, the guests were served with a cream cheese made from either cow's milk or ewe's milk. Then they got apples, nuts and honey. At the high table they drank fine wines. If the feast was in England, these wines were imported from France.

Entertainment

A Norman baron or lord had no problems in finding someone to entertain his guests at a feast. If he was very rich, he might employ his own jester to do tricks and tell jokes. There were also entertainers who travelled around the countryside. The entertainers included groups of **minstrels,** jugglers and acrobats. There were men with performing monkeys and bears that danced to music. Towards the end of the Norman period groups of **jongleurs** and **troubadours** sang romantic songs to the music of a guitar.

▽ **To entertain his guests** a Norman baron would hire groups of musicians for the evening. They would perform between courses and after the meal. Sometimes people danced to the music and sometimes they sang. On the first picture, the instruments from left to right are the kettle drums, the cittern, the harp, the fiddle and the psaltery. Sometimes the baron would also hire a group of mummers to put on a mime for his guests. The mummers on the second picture have disguised themselves with animal heads.

Sports and games

Hunting was a favourite pastime of rich Normans. They liked to ride out on their horses and hunt for wild boar and other animals. It was not just a sport to them, however. It was also a way of getting a greater variety of food to eat. This was especially true in winter when the only other meat they had was that from animals that had been killed in the autumn. Poor people wanted fresh meat, too, but they were not allowed to hunt openly. Instead they had to sneak into the forests and try to kill an animal without being seen. This was known as poaching. If they were caught, they might be branded with a hot iron or blinded. They might also have their hands cut off or even be hanged.

Hawking or falconry

Rich Normans enjoyed this sport. They went on horseback and each man took his own hawk with him. The man wore a thick leather glove on one hand. The hawk perched on his hand and was fastened to the man's wrist with a leather strap. Boys and dogs also went with them. When the hunters saw birds such as partridges or herons, they sent the boys ahead to make a noise and scare the birds into flight. Then the hunters released their hawks, which swooped on the birds and killed them, as shown in this picture. Then the dogs were sent to bring the dead birds back to the hunters. After the kill, the hawk returned to its owner's wrist until it was time to fly after another bird. When enough birds had been caught, the hunters took them back to the castle or manor house where the birds were cooked and eaten.

◁ **King Harold riding out with his falcon** on his wrist — a scene from the Bayeux Tapestry.

₺ dient que for tous ses grans proeches perent
l e pris de la iornee par amor li donnerent

◁ **Guessing games** were very popular in Norman times and often both adults and children joined in. Blind Man's Buff was one of the most popular. It was also known as Hoodman Blind. In the picture three girls are teasing the 'blind man' by hitting her with knotted hoods. She has to guess which one is which.

The punishments were worst if someone was caught poaching in one of the Royal Forests in England. These were vast areas of land which William the Conqueror kept for himself. Before William's time, poor people gathered firewood from the forests. They fed their pigs there and collected wild honey. They were angry that they could not do this in the Royal Forests. Two of William's sons were killed in the New Forest in England and many people thought it was a punishment for their greed.

Competitions and races

As well as hunting, rich Normans enjoyed archery. They competed with each other to see who was the best shot with a bow and arrow. Villagers sometimes enjoyed archery contests, too. Other sports included wrestling, swimming in summer and ice-skating in winter. Manuscripts also tell of horseracing and contests to catch a pig with a soapy tail. There were also various kinds of football. One sort of game was between the people in one village played against the people in the next village. There was a goal in each village with about five to eight kilometres between them. There were no rules and no set length of time for the game. The game often got violent and many people were hurt.

△ **An early form of cricket.** This picture from a twelfth century manuscript shows a group of men playing a game of cryc. It was first played by shepherds who turned their crooks upside down and used them to hit a ball or other round object. When other people started playing, they also used a stick shaped like a shepherd's crook. Cryc developed over the years into the modern game of cricket.

A tournament

When there were no enemies to fight against, the Normans had mock battles, or **tournaments,** between themselves. The tournaments of the eleventh century were often arranged by rich **barons**. The barons made up the rules and gave the prizes for the winners. By the twelfth century, tournaments were so popular that knights would travel a long way to take part in one. Some went to show that they were loyal to their lord. Others went as **freelances**. They fought for a baron they did not know. This was because a knight could make large sums of money from winning a tournament.

On the day of the tournament, spectators gathered at a place chosen by the person who had arranged the tournament. The knights came with their squires.

◁ **A tournament scene,** showing knights on horseback charging at each other with lances. To prevent serious injury, they aim at each other's shields, rather than at each other's bodies. Some of the lances that have broken earlier in the tournament are on the ground. The winner will be the knight who stays on his horse the longest. Because many knights were killed or injured in tournaments, new rules were invented late in the thirteenth century to make tournaments safer. No knight could bring more than three squires with him and no prisoners could be taken for ransom. Sharp weapons were banned and there was a group of stewards to make sure these rules were obeyed.

I i foffe font parfont ꝛ li terrail font droit

These were young men who were training to be knights. At a tournament they helped a knight by looking after his weapons and horses. The knights wore badges on their shields and on their surcoats so they could tell who was on their side and who was on the other. They lined up facing each other. Then a signal was given and the tournament began. The tournament might last a few days and move around the countryside as the fighting went on. Sometimes even the spectators joined in. Some knights were killed and many more injured. Some were also taken prisoner and held for ransom.

Many popes were against tournaments. They thought the knights should be fighting in the **Crusades** instead. Some knights were against tournaments, too. They were worried in case one of the barons built up a strong army of knights and went to war against the crown. Other knights saw tournaments as a way of making money and they made the barons pay a sum of money to hold a tournament.

Most knights saw tournaments as good practice for real battles. Roger of Howden, an Englishman who lived in Norman times, wrote: 'A knight cannot do well in war if he has not prepared for it in tournaments. He must have seen his own blood flow. He must have had his teeth crunched under the blow of his opponent.'

◁ **A villein tilting at a quintain.** This was made from two pieces of wood, joined together in a T-shape. The cross-bar was on a pivot so that it could turn around. At one end of it there was a board with a target and at the other end there was a heavy bag of sand. The villein ran at the quintain and tilted it with a wooden pole. This made the sandbag swing round and, if the villein did not run past fast enough, the sandbag would knock him over. A knight also practised tilting at the quintain, but he charged up to it on horseback and used a lance to hit the target. If he did not ride past fast enough, the sandbag would knock him off his horse. Because his armour was so heavy, a knight found it difficult to get up again once he had fallen.

△ **This man is having an arrow removed** from his back by a surgeon. In Norman times there were no pain-killing drugs, and ointments were made of things like chopped-up beetles mixed with fat. Medicines were made from herbs, dead insects and powdered rocks. Nobody knew about keeping wounds clean and so a wounded knight was more likely to die from his treatment than from his injuries.

Norman knights

The son of a **baron** or a lord started training to be a knight when he was about eight or nine years old. At that age his father usually sent him to live at the castle of an uncle or a cousin. The boy would have a tutor to teach him Latin and French, but he would spend most of his time in exercise and practical work. He looked after the horses and acted as a servant, or a page, to the knight who was training him. At the dinner table, he had to go on bended knee to pass the lord his wine cup. There were strict rules about this and about general behaviour at the table. Some of these rules were written down. They included, 'Do not sit down until you are told to' and 'Do not drink with a full mouth'. A page was also told 'Do not pick your nose, teeth or nails, or put so much in your mouth that you cannot answer when spoken to'.

By the time he was 14 a page was supposed to be good at **fencing**, hunting, hawking, riding a horse and **tilting** at the **quintain**. If he could do all these things, he qualified to be a squire. His training went on for five or six more years as he went with his lord to tournaments and on visits to other castles. Then, when he was about 20, a squire was made into a knight.

◁ **A kite-shaped shield** gave the best protection to a knight on horseback as it protected his body without getting in his way. This carving of a Norman knight on horseback is in the cathedral at Monreale in Sicily. The Normans spent many years breeding a special sort of horse to carry them into battle. It had to be very strong to carry the weight of a man and his armour. It also had to be quick and agile so that it could get itself and its rider out of danger. The horses that were finally used were called destriers.

Battle dress

When they were fighting, Norman knights were protected by a suit of chain mail. This was made up of hundreds of small steel rings and made to measure by an armourer. It was very heavy and a knight needed his squire to help him get dressed for a battle. First he put on leggings, or chausses, of chain mail. Then he put on a padded jacket, or gambeson, which came almost to his knees. Over this he wore a hauberk, which was a long-sleeved shirt of chain mail and also came almost to his knees. On his head, he wore a skull cap. He then put on a coif. This was a hood of chain mail which covered his head and neck. Just before the battle started, he put on his heavy helmet and his chain mail gloves. With so much protective clothing, very few knights were killed in battle unless they fell off their horses. More died after the battle from infected wounds and fevers.

Foot soldiers were thought to be unimportant, except in siege warfare and for duties around the camp. Because of this, their only protection was a basin-shaped helmet and a padded tunic or leather jacket.

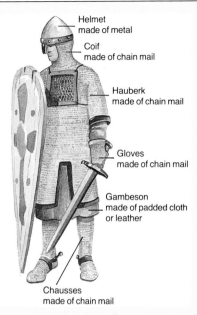

Helmet
made of metal

Coif
made of chain mail

Hauberk
made of chain mail

Gloves
made of chain mail

Gambeson
made of padded cloth
or leather

Chausses
made of chain mail

△ **A Norman knight.**

Knights on horseback

Norman knights could fight on horseback, and this is what made them so successful. Before the time of the Normans, soldiers had ridden their horses as far as the battlefield and then got off and fought on foot. The Bayeux Tapestry, however, shows the Norman knights riding their horses into battle. They could do this because of three inventions. The first was the stirrup, which meant that the knight could mount and dismount quickly. The second was the high-backed saddle which held the knight firmly on his horse. The third was the long **lance** made of ash-wood. If the enemy was on foot and fighting with a sword or battleaxe, a knight on horseback could knock him down with the lance without being hit himself. One **medieval** writer said that the Normans fighting on horseback 'could smash a hole in the walls of Babylon'.

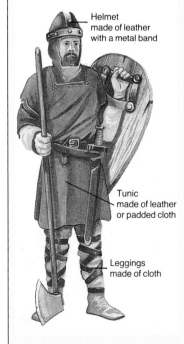

Helmet
made of leather
with a metal band

Tunic
made of leather
or padded cloth

Leggings
made of cloth

△ **A Norman footsoldier.**

Siege warfare

A Norman knight was hard to beat in a **pitched battle,** but Normans did not always fight this way. Sometimes they **besieged** their enemy in his castle. When this happened, the foot soldiers and the archers did most of the work.

Attacking a castle

The Normans besieged a castle by surrounding it completely. This made sure that the people inside could not get food from outside. Then they used different weapons to try and break into the castle or force the enemy to come out.

The simplest weapon was the battering ram made from the trunk of a tree. The soldiers used it to try and knock down the castle gate. While they did this, they sheltered under a tortoise. This was a large frame covered with sheets of hide or metal. It protected the men from the stones or whatever else the enemy dropped on them.

The Normans attacked castle walls with a metal bore, called a mouse. This chipped at a stone until it came loose. Then they pulled the stone out and moved the mouse to the next one. If enough stones came out, the wall collapsed and the attackers could rush into the castle.

Another way of making a wall collapse was by

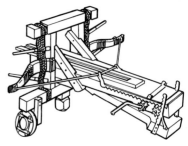

△ **The ballista** was like a giant crossbow on a heavy wooden frame. The bow was pulled back by a rope, and a large arrow or bolt was slotted into position. This bolt was often tipped with a mixture that burnt easily, called 'Greek Fire'. When the bolt was released, the attackers hoped it would go over the castle wall and set fire to something inside.

◁ **This picture of the siege of Antioch** was drawn in the late thirteenth century. It is one of the earliest attempts to show what a siege was really like. The siege of Antioch was part of the First Crusade, however, and the Crusaders then dressed differently from the ones in this picture. They wore suits of mail covered by a linen coat to keep out the heat and the glare of the sun. Shields with painted lions and other animals are also from the thirteenth century.

digging a tunnel underneath it. While the attackers were working on the tunnel, they held its roof up with wooden props. When they finished it, they filled it with leaves and branches soaked with grease to make them burn easily. The attackers set the leaves and branches on fire, and when the fire burned through the props, the wall fell down.

The attackers also used weapons called mangonels and trebuchets to hurl large stones over the castle walls. Sometimes they also threw the bodies of dead horses over the walls and hoped that these would spread disease among the people inside.

Defending a castle

The Normans built their castles so as to make them easy to defend against an enemy. Archers could shelter behind the battlements on the outer wall to fire arrows on the attackers. Towers had narrow windows which made it easy to fire an arrow out, but difficult to fire one in.

Once the drawbridge across the moat was lifted, it was difficult for the attackers to get close to the castle. The people inside the castle threw stones and rubbish over the walls at them. Some castles had towers with machicolations. These were slots cut into the floor of a platform which stuck out near the top of the tower. The defenders used them to pour boiling water and blazing fat straight down onto the attackers.

If the defenders had enough food and water, a siege could last for many months. At first knights who gave their lord 40 days' service a year were allowed to leave the siege when the 40 days were over. Later some knights gave their lord a sum of money instead of doing knight-service. The lord then paid **mercenary** knights to fight for him.

△ **A belfry.** If the attackers could not knock the castle walls down, they tried to climb over them using a siege tower or belfry. This was on wheels and could be pushed up to the castle wall. Animal skins or sheets of wood on the outside of the belfry protected the attackers while they climbed up the ladders inside.

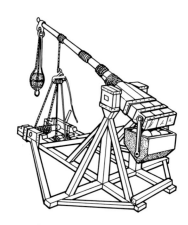

△ **The trebuchet** was a siege weapon like a giant see-saw with a sling at one end. When a large weight was dropped on the other end whatever was in the sling was thrown over the enemy's walls.

The Normans in France

When King Charles the Simple of France made his treaty with the Vikings in 911, he gave them land in and around Rouen. In exchange, they had to help him defend France from other Viking raiders. They also had to become Christian. Their leader, Rollo, had to marry the king's daughter, Giselle. Although Rollo was their leader, however, his men did not think he was any more important than they were. When the French asked them the name of their lord, they said, 'He has no name for we are all equal in power'.

While Rollo and his men settled in the area around Rouen, other Vikings moved to live in western Normandy. Some of them were Danes who had lived in England and others were Norwegians who had lived in Scotland and Ireland. Most of these settlers were men. Like Rollo and his followers, they married local women and their language and way of living soon became more French than Viking.

Over the years the King of France gave more land to Rollo and his followers. When Rollo died in the

△ **The Norman monasteries,** like this one at Cerisy le Foret, France, were centres of learning. History, medicine, poetry and music were studied there, as well as religion. Rollo and his followers originally became Christians to please the King of France, and also kept their old gods for a long time. It was only later that the Dukes became truly Christian and began to build the monasteries.

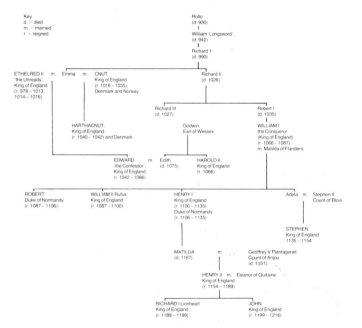

◁ **This family tree shows the Dukes of Normandy** from Rollo to John. It also shows the kings of England in the same period. The two families were connected by Emma of Normandy, who was first married to Ethelred of England and then to Cnut, who was also King of Denmark. William I was the first person to be Duke of Normandy and King of England. His great-great-grandson John was the last.

year 930 his son, William Longsword, was chosen to be the new Duke of Normandy. But 12 years later William was murdered and his young son, Richard, became the next **Duke**. Richard was known as Richard the Fearless and he was Duke of Normandy for over 50 years. When he died, his son became Duke. He was Richard II and he ruled until he died in 1026. His oldest son, also called Richard, then became Duke. He died only a year later. His younger brother, Robert the Magnificent, became Duke.

William the Conqueror

In 1028 the daughter of a **tanner** in the town of Falaise gave birth to a son. His name was William. His mother's name was Herleve. His father was Robert the Magnificent, but his parents never married. Robert died in 1035 on his way back from a pilgrimage to the Holy Land. But before he died, he had named William as the next Duke of Normandy.

Because William was still a child, he was helped by his uncle and later by the King of France and the Count of Flanders. In 1047, however, he started to rule Normandy by himself. He defeated an uprising by Guy of Burgundy and soon proved himself a good soldier and a leader of men. By 1066 he had added Maine and Britanny to the Duchy of Normandy. Then he began to think about conquering England.

△ **The Normans were descended from the Vikings** who had first started to leave their homelands of Norway, Denmark and Sweden in the late eighth century. These Vikings were famous as raiders and traders, but most of them were also farmers. One reason why they left their homelands was that there was not enough good farming land for everyone there. For example, Norway (see top) is mountainous and rocky. However, in Normandy (bottom) there was plenty of good land and Rollo shared it out among his followers. Many of them married French women and forgot the old Viking way of life.

Knights Crusader

By the eighth century the Arab followers of the Prophet Mohammed had conquered Syria, Palestine, Egypt and much of the Middle East. In spite of the differences in their religions, however, they treated the Christians and the Jews well. They also allowed Christian pilgrims from the west to visit the holy places in Jerusalem.

This changed around 1070 when Turks from central Asia overran the area. They captured Jerusalem and Palestine and threatened Constantinople, which was the centre of the Byzantine empire. They also said that any Christians

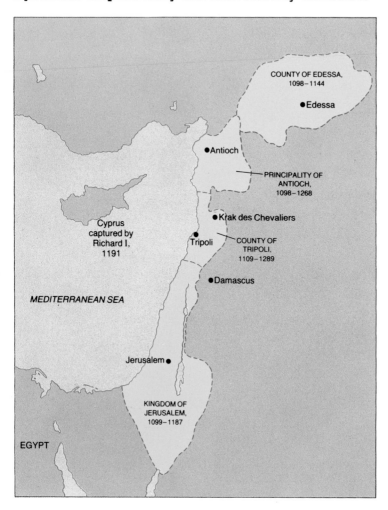

COUNTY OF EDESSA,
1098–1144

●Edessa

●Antioch

PRINCIPALITY OF
ANTIOCH,
1098–1268

●Krak des Chevaliers

Cyprus
captured by
Richard I,
1191

●
Tripoli

COUNTY OF
TRIPOLI,
1109–1289

●Damascus

MEDITERRANEAN SEA

Jerusalem ●

KINGDOM OF
JERUSALEM,
1099–1187

EGYPT

◁ **The Crusader states.**

◁ **The castle of Krak des Chevaliers** in Syria was the greatest of all the fortresses built by the Crusaders. It was on the site of a former Muslim fortress. Between 1140 and 1200 the Crusaders added the two outer walls which were separated by a wide moat. This made the castle very strong and difficult to defeat. The Knights of St John held the castle from 1142 until 1271, when it was captured by the Muslims.

who were caught on pilgrimages to Jerusalem would be killed or sold as slaves. When the Pope heard of this in 1095, he called on all Christian knights to go to Jerusalem and take it back from the Turks. The Crusades were about to begin.

In 1096 five armies set out on the First Crusade. Three were from the kingdom of France. One from Normandy was led by Robert Curthose, son of William the Conqueror. The fifth one was made up of Normans from Italy and Sicily, and was led by Robert Guiscard's son, Bohemond. They all met at Constantinople and from there set out for Jerusalem. On the way there, in 1098, Bohemond captured Antioch, in Syria, and stayed there as prince of a Norman state which was to last for almost 200 years. The rest of the Crusaders went on to Jerusalem which they captured from the Muslims in 1099.

The Second Crusade started in 1145 to try and gain more land from the Muslims. It was a failure and in 1187 Saladin led the Muslims to recapture Jerusalem. The Third Crusade started in 1190 and this time Richard the Lionheart, King of England, was one of the leaders. This crusade also ended in failure in 1192. After that the knights gave up trying to take Jerusalem from the Muslims, but the Crusades continued until the end of the thirteenth century.

△ **A great Muslim warrior.** This picture is thought to show Salah ed-Din Yusuf, who is better known as Saladin. Saladin was brought up in Damascus, but gained control over the Muslim lands in Egypt and in Syria. He was said to be short, rather plump, red-faced and blind in one eye. He was also modest, educated and a brilliant soldier. He led the Muslims against the Crusaders and captured the Kingdom of Jerusalem in 1187. He fought against the Crusaders until his death in 1193.

The Normans in Italy

Early in the eleventh century, Italy was not one country but contained many little states. These states were always fighting against each other. In 1016 some Norman pilgrims went to Jerusalem. On their way home, they landed in Apulia in southern Italy and soon realized that a good soldier could make a lot of money in the fighting there. They took this news back to Normandy and soon small groups of men set out for Italy.

In 1030 a Norman called Rannulf won land at Aversa and set up the first Norman state there. Other Normans followed his example and by 1100 they had conquered the whole of southern Italy and Sicily.

A fighting family

One family was very important in the Norman conquest of Italy. Tancred de Hauteville, who lived near Coutances in Normandy, had 12 sons. He was not very rich and so eight of his sons went to try and make a living in Italy. In 1041 they were among 300 Norman knights who came from Aversa to the hill-town of Melfi to defeat the Byzantine soldiers in Apulia. The Normans captured the towns of Venosa, Lavello and Ascoli and beat the Byzantines in three **pitched battles.** William Bras-de-Fer, one of Tancred's sons, became ruler of Apulia.

In 1059 Robert Guiscard, another son of Tancred de Hauteville, became Duke of Apulia and Calabria. This brought him near to the island of Sicily which had been ruled by Muslim Arabs, or Saracens from North Africa, for over 200 years. Robert decided to try and conquer that, too. His youngest brother Roger did most of the fighting, while Robert made plans to become leader of the Byzantine Empire which was ruled from Constantinople. Robert failed in this and died in 1085. Roger was successful in Sicily, however, and by 1091 he had conquered the whole island.

△ **Christ crowning Roger II as King of Sicily in 1130.** The picture is in the church of Santa Maria del'Ammiraglio in Palermo in Sicily. This kind of picture is called a mosaic and is made by sticking pieces of coloured stone onto a flat surface.

Roger II was the son of Roger I, and by 1140 he ruled over Calabria, Apulia, Capua and Naples, as well as Sicily. After an insult by the Byzantine emperor, Roger's admiral attacked the coasts of Dalmatia and Epirus, today part of Yugoslavia and Greece. He captured Corfu and plundered Athens and Corinth in 1146. He also captured silk-workers and took them back to Sicily to start a silk industry there. In 1147 Roger won Tripoli, Tunis and Algeria in North Africa. This expansion of his kingdom meant that he now ruled over a mixture of Christians and Muslims of many nationalities. He was a just ruler, however, and many learned men gathered around him.

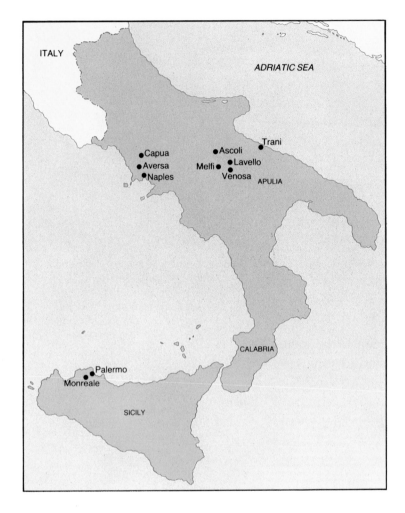

△ **The monastery at Monreale** in Sicily was built by the Normans in the twelfth century. This view shows the cloister where the monks walked for exercise.

The rounded arches and the leaves decorating the tops of the pillars are typical Norman features. The pointed arches and the zig-zag patterns on the pillars are in the Arabian style. This cloister is much lighter and more airy than cloisters in monasteries in France or England. This is because the climate in Sicily was much more sunny and so the monks did not need so much shelter from the rain and the cold.

After the Normans had gone

The Normans who settled in Italy and Sicily built monasteries, castles, churches and cathedrals. Some of these were in a mixture of styles, especially in Sicily where the influence of the Arabs was very strong. Many of them can still be seen today, such as the cathedral at Trani in Apulia, and some are still in use.

The most important thing the Normans did was to unite the little states of southern Italy and Sicily. Norman rule ended there in 1194, but the states never split up again.

William the Conqueror

When Edward the Confessor, King of England, died on 5 January 1066, three men claimed the throne. The first was Harold Godwinson, Earl of Wessex. He had been the most important man in England after Edward. He had himself crowned king on 6 January 1066, the day Edward was buried. The second man was Harald Hardrada of Norway. In August 1066 he joined forces with Harold Godwinson's brother, Tostig, and sailed to England. They captured the city of York on 20 September, but were defeated by Harold Godwinson's army at Stamford Bridge, Yorkshire, on 24 September.

William, Duke of Normandy, also claimed the throne of England. His grandfather's sister, Emma, had been married to two kings of England and was the mother of Edward the Confessor. (There is a family tree on page 50.) Edward had grown up in Normandy and kept close contact with Normandy while he was King of England. William claimed that Edward had promised the throne to him. On 27 September William set sail for England with 7000 men. Many were Normans, but there were also Bretons, Flemings and Frenchmen who hoped to make a fortune out of fighting. Harold heard the news in York on 1 October and quickly marched south. His army met William's at the Battle of Hastings on 14 October 1066. At first it seemed that Harold would win. Then he was killed and the victory went to William.

William was crowned King of England on Christmas Day, 1066. From 1067 to 1071 there were rebellions in England, especially in the North and the Midlands. By 1069, in what was called 'The Harrying of the North', William was dealing with these brutally — by destroying villages, crops and cattle and leaving people to starve. The last rebellion was crushed in 1071 when William defeated Hereward the Wake at the Isle of Ely.

△ **The castle at Falaise in Normandy.** William the Conqueror was born at Falaise around the year 1028. His father was Robert, Duke of Normandy. His mother was called Herleve and she was the daughter of a tanner in Falaise. Robert and Herleve were never married. Because of this, William was probably born at the home of Herleve's parents and not at the castle.

◁ **Harold's oath.** This scene from the Bayeux Tapestry shows Harold Godwinson with William, Duke of Normandy, at the castle of Bayeux. Harold has one hand on an altar and the other hand on a box of holy relics. William claimed that when Harold did this, he promised he would accept William as his king after the death of Edward the Confessor. No one knows whether this was true or not, but William made people believe that it was. He even made the Pope believe it and the Pope sent him a holy flag and some holy relics to take with him to England.

William's sons

There were also rebellions in Normandy while William was in England. Some were led by his oldest son, Robert Curthose. Robert was also involved in disputes about the boundaries of Normandy. On 9 September 1087 William died at Rouen. In his will he named Robert as Duke of Normandy and his favourite son, William Rufus, as King of England. His youngest son, Henry, was given money. In 1095 Robert lent Normandy to William Rufus in exchange for money and went away on the First Crusade. William was killed while he was hunting in the New Forest before Robert returned, and in 1100 Henry declared himself King of England and Duke of Normandy.

▽ **Norman soldiers landing at Pevensey** in Sussex, England, after their crossing from St Valery-sur-Somme. As well as bringing horses, food and weapons, the Normans also brought wood, nails and carpenters' tools to build three forts. The day after they landed, they built the first of these forts inside the ruins of the Roman fortress at Pevensey and moved all their stores there. Pevensey was only a small place, however, and next day William and some of his men set out to look for somewhere bigger. They found Hastings and quickly built the other two forts there. The army of 7000 men then moved from Pevensey to Hastings to wait for news of Harold. While they waited, they raided the area for food and other supplies. Other scenes on the Bayeux tapestry show them killing local people and burning houses.

The Angevin Empire

William the Conqueror's son, Henry, had two children. One was a son called William, but he was drowned in a shipwreck in 1120. The other was a daughter called Matilda. She married the Emperor of Germany. When he died, Matilda married Geoffrey, Duke of Anjou. Henry wanted Matilda to come to the throne after he died in 1135. Instead his nephew, Stephen of Blois, took the throne while Matilda was in Normandy. Stephen was very popular, but he was not a strict ruler and soon the English barons were doing whatever they wanted. They built castles, declared war on each other and held prisoners to ransom. In 1139 Matilda tried to take the throne, but she was unpopular and did not succeed. Matilda's son, Henry of Anjou, invaded England in 1153. A civil war seemed likely. Then Stephen's son, Eustace, died suddenly and Henry became Stephen's heir.

Henry became King of England in 1154 and was the first of the Angevin kings. He ruled over more territory than any of the English kings before him, but towards the end of his reign his empire started to break up. When Henry died in 1189 his son, Richard, succeeded him. Richard was killed in 1199 and his brother, John, inherited the Angevin empire. John soon lost Anjou, Maine and Touraine to his nephew, Arthur of Britanny. Then in 1204 he lost Normandy to the French King, Philip Augustus. In England, John was always short of money and nobody trusted him. He tried to regain Normandy in 1214 but did not succeed. When he died in 1216, the Anglo-Norman age was finally over.

What the Normans left us

Over 700 years after the Norman age ended, there is still plenty to remind us of how important the Normans were in the history of the places where they lived. There are castles that remind us that the

△ **This figure of Henry II** is on his tomb at Fontevrault in France. As well as being King of England and Duke of Normandy, he also ruled over the lands belonging to his wife, Eleanor of Aquitaine. This gave him an empire which stretched from Scotland to the south of France. However, during Henry's reign the barons started thinking of themselves as French or English, rather than Norman. His sons rebelled against him, and Richard, who came to the throne after Henry's death in 1189, was more interested in going on a crusade than in ruling his empire. Less than 30 years after Henry's death, the Angevin empire had broken up and Normandy and England were ruled separately.

◁ **Chateau Gaillard on the River Seine in Normandy.** Richard I built this castle in 1195-8 to try and defend his territory. The castle was well designed, but the Angevin empire lost control of Normandy while Richard's brother John was king. Chateau Gaillard surrendered to Philip Augustus, King of France, in 1204, after six months of siege.

Normans were great fighters and there are many Norman churches that remind us that the Normans encouraged the Christian religion wherever they went.

The Vikings who first went to Normandy gave Scandinavian names to places where they settled — such as Gaudebec and Yvetot. Their descendants who came to England in 1066 spoke French, however, and gave England place-names such as Beaulieu and Richmond. They also added French words to the English language.

The Normans were good organizers and some of their ideas about governing a country are still used today. They were the first rulers in Europe to keep a record of who owned what, and they had a well-organized tax system. When they came to England, they found that the Anglo-Saxons already had a good system of law. The Normans improved on this and, in the reign of Henry II, they started a system called Common Law. This meant that the law was the same for all men in all places. Although the laws themselves have changed over the centuries, Henry II's system of Common Law is the basis for Law today in the United States and the Commonwealth.

△ **King John and the Magna Carta.** By 1215 King John was so unpopular with the English barons that many of them were prepared to fight against him. To try and avoid a war, they asked the king to meet them on 15 June at Runnymede, an island in the River Thames. There he put his seal to the Articles of the Barons. This was a draft of the Magna Carta, which gave rights to the barons. However, in spite of the Magna Carta, civil war broke out and only ended when John died.

Time line

911   The King of France gives land around Rouen to Rollo, the Viking leader. Rollo and his men settle down and the land becomes known as Normandy.

930   Rollo dies and his son, William Longsword, is chosen as next Duke of Normandy.

1027   Robert the Magnificent, a great-great-grandson of Rollo, becomes Duke of Normandy.

1028   Birth of William, son of Robert the Magnificent.

1030   Rannulf sets up the first Norman state in Italy at Aversa.

1035   Robert the Magnificent dies. William becomes Duke of Normandy at the age of 7.

1041   William Bras-de-Fer, a Norman, becomes ruler of Apulia in Italy.

1047   William the Conqueror starts to rule Normandy by himself and defeats Guy of Burgundy at the battle of Val-es-Dunes.

1059   Robert Guiscard becomes Duke of Apulia and Calabria.

1066   5 January: Death of Edward the Confessor, King of England.
6 January: Harold Godwinson is crowned King of England.
20 September: Harald Hardrada, King of Norway, captures York, in England.
24 September: Harold of England defeats and kills Harald Hardrada at Stamford Bridge, Yorkshire, in England.
27 September: William of Normandy sets sail for England with 7000 men.
14 October: After marching from Stamford Bridge, Harold and his army are defeated near Hastings by William's army.
25 December: William is crowned King of England in Westminster Abbey.

1067 – 69   Rebellions in the north of England against William the Conqueror.

1069 – 70   'The Harrying of the North' – William destroys crops, cattle and villages in northern England.

1070   The Turks capture Jerusalem.

1071   William the Conqueror crushes the last English rebellion when he defeats Hereward the Wake.

1086   The Domesday Survey is carried out.

1087   On 9 September William dies in Normandy. William Rufus becomes King of England. Robert Curthose becomes Duke of Normandy.

1091   Roger de Hauteville conquers Sicily.

1095   The Pope calls on all Christian knights to go to Jerusalem and take it back from the Turks.

1096   The First Crusade starts. Robert lends Normandy to William Rufus in exchange for money and goes to Jerusalem.

1098	Robert Guiscard's son, Bohemond, captures Antioch.	1153	Henry invades England. Stephen agrees to make him his heir.
1099	The Crusaders capture Jerusalem.	1154	Stephen dies and Henry II becomes the first Angevin King of England.
1100	William Rufus is killed. His brother, Henry, becomes King of England.	1187	The Muslim leader, Saladin, takes Jerusalem from the Christians.
1101	Robert Curthose, William's son, invades England because he thinks he should be king.	1189	Henry's sons rebel against him. He dies at Chinon in France and his son Richard becomes King of England.
1106	Henry defeats Robert Curthose at the Battle of Tinchebray and becomes Duke of Normandy as well as King of England.	1190 – 92	Richard I goes on the Third Crusade. It also ends in failure.
1120	Henry's only son, William, drowns in a shipwreck.	1193	Saladin dies.
1128	Henry's daughter, Matilda, marries Geoffrey of Anjou.	1193 – 4	Richard in prison in Germany. He is only released on payment of a huge ransom.
1135	Henry I dies. His daughter Matilda is not popular in England and her cousin Stephen becomes king.	1194	Norman rule ends in Italy and Sicily.
1139 – 53	Civil war in England between Stephen's supporters and Matilda's supporters.	1199	Richard I dies in a siege in France. His brother John becomes king.
1141 – 5	Geoffrey of Anjou conquers Normandy.	1203 – 4	Philip Augustus, King of France, conquers Anjou and Normandy.
1145	The Second Crusade sets out to Jerusalem but does not gain any more land.	1214	King John of England tries to regain Normandy at the battle of Bouvines, but he is defeated.
1147	Roger II of Sicily wins land in North Africa.	1215	The English barons force John to sign the Magna Carta. Civil war breaks out in England.
1152	Matilda's son, Henry of Anjou, marries Eleanor of Aquitaine and gains her vast lands.	1216	John dies. The civil war ends.

Glossa

glossary

anvil: a block o
on which the bla
metal into shape

apprentice: a yo
trade by working .... craftsman

archaeologist: a person who tries to find out what happened in the past by finding and studying old buildings and objects

artefact: an object that was made by people in the past

bailiff: a man whose job it was to keep law and order in a particular area

baron: one of the king's tenants-in-chief. He held large areas of land. In return, he helped the king to defend his kingdom

besiege: to attack a town or a castle by surrounding it so that no one could get in or out

bordar: a peasant who lived on a manor and farmed about 2 hectares of land. He was better off than a cottar, but still had to work one day each week for his lord

burgess: someone who lived in a town and had the right to elect a mayor

come of age: to be thought of as an adult. In Norman times this usually happened about 14

common land: land which could be used by everyone in the village

cottar: a peasant who lived on a manor and farmed about 2 hectares of land. In exchange, he worked for his lord for at least one day each week

crusade: a campaign by Christian knights (**Crusaders**) who came from all parts of Europe to try and recapture the Holy Land from the Muslims

demesne: (pronounced *demean*) the land belonging to the manor which was worked for the lord

diocese: the area ruled over by a bishop. Its centre is a large church or cathedral

dowry: the gifts from a bride's family to a bridegroom on their marriage

duke: a man who was almost as important as a king. He ruled over a small state which was called a **duchy**

excavation: the careful digging up of buried objects to find information about the past

fencing: the sport of fighting with a long sword

feudalism or **feudal system:** a system in which the king owned all the land. Everyone else held land from him, or from his tenants-in-chief, or from their lords of the manor. In exchange, everyone had to give some sort of service to the person they held the land from

freelances: knights who fought in tournaments to make money, and not out of loyalty to a lord

freeman: someone who held his land from the lord of the manor by paying a rent. He was free to go where he wanted without asking his lord for permission

guild: a group of merchants or craftsmen in a town. They made rules on wages and prices and said who could call himself a craftsman

jongleur: one of a group of musicians who travelled around the country and performed at castles and fairs

knight: a well-armed soldier who fought on horseback for a baron for 40 days a year, in exchange for a piece of land

lance: a weapon with a long wooden shaft and a pointed metal end

linen: a strong cloth made from the fibres of the flax plant

manor: a piece of land held by a lord. Part of it was his demesne land, the rest was farmed by peasants

mason: a person who is skilled in working with stone

mayor: the most important burgess in a Norman town

medieval: belonging to the Middle Ages. It is used to describe a period in history from the end of the Roman Empire in AD 395 until the end of the fifteenth century

mercenary: a knight who fought for money, and not out of loyalty to his lord

minstrel: someone who entertained people by playing an instrument and singing songs, or by reciting poetry he had written

misericord: a very small seat, like a shelf, which the monks could lean on when they had to stand for a long time

motte-and-bailey castle: a type of castle built by the Normans on a mound of earth (the motte). The motte was surrounded by an enclosed area (the bailey)

parish: an area of land which had its own church and its own priest

peasant: a person who worked the land for someone else. Peasants were the biggest group of people in Norman society, but they had the least wealth and the least power

pewter: a grey metal made from a mixture of tin and lead

pitched battle: a battle that has been planned in advance, with the soldiers arranged in an orderly way and the two armies facing each other

quintain: a T-shaped post with a shield on one end and a sandbag on the other. Knights practised tilting against it

rushlight: a candle made by dipping the inside of a rush, (a waterplant) into grease that would burn

serf: a person who owned nothing and had very few legal rights

sheriff: the man who represented the king's authority in a county

spit: a metal rod on which meat or fish is skewered and roasted over the fire

stew: a pond where people kept fish to eat

strip: one of the pieces of land farmed by a peasant in the Open Field system

tanner: someone who makes leather

tapestry: a form of embroidery on a woven background. Tapestries made in Norman times often told a story

tilting: thrusting with a lance or a pole at another knight or at a quintain

toll: a sum of money which outsiders had to pay to go over a bridge, or come into a town to trade

tournament: in Norman times this was a mock battle between two groups of knights. There were few rules and many people were killed or badly hurt

treaty: an agreement between two important countries, or people

trencher: a wooden board on which food such as meat was served

troubadour: a travelling singer or poet who made up romantic songs and poetry

vassal: a man who recognized a lord as his master, often in exchange for land and protection

villein: a peasant who farmed around 12 hectares of land on a manor. In exchange, he had to work 2 or 3 days a week for his lord

Index